FROM MY WINDOWED CORNER

Also by Frances Johnston Nash

Lord, I'm Listening…..
but <u>sometimes</u> I squawk!
A Personal Devotion
of Christian Growth

FROM
MY
WINDOWED
CORNER

Poems

Frances Johnston Nash

Amelia Island Publishing
Amelia Island, Florida
2008

Library of Congress Control Number
2008937610

ISBN-13: 978-0-9748086-7-3

Dust Jacket Design by Latitudes

Amelia Island Publishing, Inc.
Amelia Island, Florida
info@ameliapublishing.com

Printed in the United States of America

While Giving Thanks

In early day I look to You,
    and thanks begin to rise.
Thanks for all You've done for me,
    for changes You have wrought.

While giving thanks in new born day,
    I sense a subtle change.
My thanks begin to bring me joy,
    to grow and then to glow.

Soon they start to ring with praise,
    clear as crystal bells.
The praises grow and chime and sing
    'til Jesus gives me strength
    for whatever day may bring.

F.N.

ACKNOWLEDGEMENTS

I truly wanted to write this book but I needed encouragement because doubt kept staring me in the eye with its intimidating gaze.

The following people came to my rescue with reassurance and I am grateful: my daughter Kakie Roberts; husband E. William Nash, Jr.; Lou Beck, a forever friend and Betty Bedell, friend, photographer and editor. Whenever my enthusiasm sagged they propped it up.

Lou and Kakie read the script and offered good suggestions. Ted Schroder, pastor and author, saw to its publishing. Dick Buck, good neighbor, friend and computer expert, rescued me from the frustrating tentacles of my many armed computer time after time. Anita Fish, a lovely new friend was also helpful.

Thanks to all you dear, generous people. I ask our mutual and astonishing Father in Heaven to bless and keep each of you.

IN MEMORIAM

Many of the poems in this book have come as a result of living with my original family: father, Dr. Harry Buchanan Johnston, DDS, who discovered and established Endodonture, known colloquially and internationally as root canal; mother, Katherine Akers Johnston; siblings, Martha Johnston Languirand; Dr. Harry Buchanan Johnston, Jr. DDS, MD; and Katherine Johnston Petty.

They are gone now to a better place. Being the last one this side of eternity leaves me with a nostalgic lonesomeness softened by hundreds of bright memories weaving themselves through my gift of a current and ever growing family.

Therefore, with pleasure, deep love and thanks, I dedicate *From my Windowed Corner* to the memory of my parents and siblings.

PREFACE

This small book of poems is a big surprise to me. I'm not even sure what makes a poem a poem. Yet here are a number which flowed from my pen. Dr. Eugene Peterson believes poetry isn't the language of objective explanation but the language of imagination. It makes an image of reality which invites our participation. Its purpose is to give us an experience. It must say something indicative about a reality common to all of us.

The name of the book is derived from unrelated things. First are the windows where my corner walls meet. Although I cannot always go outside to see the world, windows bring the world in to me, sunrise, sunset, blazing, sunny days, howling storms and placid blue river or an angry, pewter one, determined to leap its bulkhead. There's a chair in my corner. It's a strange looking contraption, called a geriatric chair. I call it Gerry. Gerry is tall. He can tip me back and lift my feet with a smooth shifting of gears. It's here, sitting in Gerry's lap that I do most of my writing, thinking and praying. Here heart and mind do their dance of joy and shed a few tears.

I am enjoying my eighty-three years. Certainly, they are heavy at times, but I think mine is a wonderful time of life … maybe even life's crown. I ask myself why I think this way when most contemporaries don't agree with me. After trying to condense happenings, both good and bad, mistakes and success, peace and war, I think my delight and contentment can be put into at least three categories. Each category has been a ribbon of growing light through the decades: God and His astonishing mercy; my family and its heart warming   individuals; earth, sky   and   water   illustrating   their incomparable beauty. The last two gifts flow from the first … God's mercy.

God and family remind me of the small beginnings in life's experience, each beginning a tiny trickle of recognizable joy.   As years multiply the trickle becomes a fresh brook bubbling its way through my consciousness with green growing things on its banks. More years, more volume develop a river dividing into numerous tributaries covering the landscape of my living. When this happens, when a life is crowded with joy, what can one do? The joy must be shared. It is pressed out of me with undeniable force and I share it through writing.

CONTENTS

Hello Self

Hello, Self, are you wondering
        why your many blessings?
Does it occur to you to look beyond
        aches, pains and daily chores
into the wondrous mysteries of mercy
        to inventory the ubiquitous *why me?*

Why not bless those who love and give
        through years of endless patience?
Why for me, Lord, do You brighten
        my weariness with rainbow colors
        of forgiveness?
Why fill my fading memory
        with fragrance of Your peace?
Why lift the burden of my years
        with this dance of hope?

Self, listen, think and wonder
        how does it happen, that I,
among earth's hurting millions,
        should know Your blessedness?
I have no answer other than my 'yes'
        to Your astonishing invitation:
"Whosoever will may come to Me."

A Single Stem

Lord, Creator, Almighty Provider, thank You!
You set us in families, clusters,
    like grapes from a single stem.
You gave me a son so dear to my soul,
    heart of my heart. Common genes
    from ancestors long ago.

I love him in joy. I love him in pain and
    longing. Thank You!
But Lord, he doesn't understand.
His spirit sleeps on. He cannot take You into
    himself as one takes nourishment.

My son hasn't met You as Bread that lives within,
    new every morning,
    fresh every evening.

I pray You my God, whose name is Holy,
    pursue him as Heaven's Hound
    through life's valleys, over its crags,
    until he falls at Your feet
    in astonished joy.

Plant him beside Your river of Life
    to flourish and grow.
You set us in families, clusters, like grapes
    from a single stem.
Please, Lord, Creator, Almighty Provider,
    make us truly one in You. Thank You.

Leaving Fingerprints

Years flash by at an astonishing rate.
Were past years really mine
    or did I simply sleep
    and remember parts of a dream?

Could this be the eighty-second year
    of my dream? Do they last that long?
Which speaks more truly, mind or body,
    concerning worth of life's events?

Body tells its up-to-date story by
    dimming eye and weakening limb.
Memory speaks only of yesterday …
    youth, maturity and vanished years.

I pray active memories of my living
    or dying may nudge others,
leaving fingerprints on growing hearts,
    proving or disproving any lasting worth.
What will remain as the result of my years?

My Windowed Corner

It's the day after Christmas. I'm tired;
    this creature isn't stirring.
I'm resting, reviewing the many
    blessings of yesterday,
      seeing loved faces, hearing joy,
      sensing God's love.

This cozy windowed corner
    brings day's outside inside to me.
The scene is quiet, veiled,
    monochromed in grays.
No visible line of demarcation
    separates river from sky.

Obscuring mists, thickly white
    tiptoe down river,
    like disembodied ghosts
    from some imponderable dream.
Weariness, plus lack of need,
    nudges me to *be* rather than *do*.

So Lord, I am in Your Presence,
    resting in Your mercy.
Though unvoiced, the realization
    lifts burdensome fatigue,
    bringing faith, brightening hope
    surrounded by love.

January Sketches

Cold and snowy, glittering white,
    or darkly gray with bitter bite.
Days grow short; nights linger longer,
    mercury drops in the thermometer.
Waterford etchings on window pane,
    wind whistles a shrill refrain.
Shadows crouch beneath each tree
    till fading light sets them free.

Sparrows fluffed against the coldness,
    wait and watch with cheeky boldness.
Crimson faces, fingers blue,
    runny noses … could be flu?
Coats buttoned snug, chins pulled low,
    snow piled high on each chapeau.

Home's blazing hearths, radiating heat,
    steaming chocolate a fragrant treat.
Sparks fly up on velvet smoke
    calling up dreams memories evoke.

Snug with warmth I watch content
    the frigid storm with wonderment.
My shivering body at last grows warm.
    and I can appreciate winter's charm.

A Bold Signature
A paraphrase of Psalm 65

All creation bears Your bold signature, identifying You,
    O Lord, as Creator, Owner, Sustainer of existence.
You are the hope of all ages, covering earth
    with the glowing garment of life.
Distant seas sparkle in Your light,
    teeming with an astonishment of creatures.

Tides lift and drop to the rhythm of Your laws.
Mountains push up and stand firm at Your command.
Seasons come, each with its particular beauty,
    following one another in orderly parade,
    year after year, according to earth's needs.
Overflowing rivers seasonally enrich the soil,
    bringing abundant crops.

Spring comes, You water Your world with rain.
Living things are blessed with refreshment and growth.
Wilderness blooms and hills are clothed in green.
Trees clap hands and dance to rhythm of breezes.
Fattening flocks dot the meadows
    and valleys ripple with ripening grain.

Events speak no words but their message is clear
    and their praise is contagious.
Let all Your creation, Lord, be it human, animal,
    mineral or vegetable, praise You
    as each fulfills Your assigned purpose.

Childish Insight

I'm only five but Auntie is eighty.
Sometimes we play lady, she in chic dresses,
    I in feather boa and clomping high heels.
Auntie needs glasses but always says, "No!"
Her face has pleats like my Sunday skirt
    and rouge gathers in its creases.

I ask my mother why Auntie looks odd,
    with bright red cheeks, round as a quarter,
    why a side of her lip swoops higher?
With hair so white, why coal black brows?
Mother's smile is gentle, both amused and sad.
She is forty-five. But I'm only five.

Mother names reasons, says Auntie is old,
She cannot see to paint within the lines.
I ask about her eyes, so milky and pale.
She says something like 'cat on a rack.'
Glasses would help but Auntie says, "No!
They make me look older."

Glasses wouldn't make Auntie look older.
They might make her look better.
Her mouth could be even, cheeks not so streaky.
She could see to color within the lines.
No, Auntie's fear is seeing the truth.
She would see what's in the mirror.

Childish Honesty

A child younger than I
    sits on Auntie's lap one day.
Looking up in childish wonder
    at rouge, wrinkles and faded eyes,
She asks, "Auntie, how old are you?
    You must be *very* old."
With angry scowl Auntie stands up,
    setting the child firmly down.

Wise counsel later advises
    the inexperienced tot,
"Never. Never tell Auntie
    she looks old.
She'd rather die than hear it!"

Now the little one, filled with advice,
    rests a hand on Auntie's knee.
With beautiful eyes, guileless as morning,
    she apologizes,
"Auntie, you're not old. You're not
    a te-ee-ny, weeny bit old ...
    but you sure are wrinkled!"

Once Again, Lord. Once Again

Today deep concern wakes me up
    covering my joy with dread's leaden hand,
    submerging me in fear.
Where does faith go when fear knocks on my door?

I tell myself, "Self, go ... be with the morning.
Sit on the balcony among geraniums,
    bougainvillea and rosemary.
Leave your fear beside the empty coffee pot.
It will wait for you if you decide to accept it again."

I go, looking into an early sky lightly touched
    by wispy cloud and pale transparent moon,
the river beneath me flows with gentle whisper,
    spreading its blueness across the spectrum.

Sun, wind, tide and circling bird add color,
    setting the day in motion.
The huge magnolia with hundreds of blooms
    in her hair is being tickled by playful breezes
    until she shivers with carefree giggles
    spilling fragrance through the air.

My soul, a dry sponge, soaks in day's beauty
    painted by Creator God, who loves me.
A sense of peace cuts me free of my burden of fear.
He whose "eye is on the sparrow" has once again
    replaced noisome doubt with comforting trust.
Once again, Lord, thank You. Once again.

Justice Rendered

A cat, imperious and still,
    watches intently from her window sill.
A crisis is building, a moment
    of sweet retribution.
Twitching tail and glittering eyes
    divulge her furtive intention.

An old dog sprawled, asleep on the floor
    basking in sunshine, feels secure.
Snoring deeply, he dreams no more.
Knowing his love for afternoon naps,
    cat plans her attack while safe on her sill.

Feline projectile is launched with a screech.
Dog's eyes pop open a moment too late.
Yelping, he scrambles, but still within reach.
Yesterday dog chased cat straight up a tree
    and today he pays double.
If she can sink claws in his vulnerable nose
    justice is rendered by small fierce cat.

Lord of the Morning

Look out the window. Morning's a'borning!
Color is rising from sky and from sea.
Sun stretches a pathway over the water,
    birds have their flutes out,
    announcing the day.

People are waking, joyful or grumpy,
    making decisions. Which shall it be?
What may I give or what can I get?
 Praising or scheming, which shall it be?

God's in His heaven projecting His glory,
    shining it through sunrise and sea,
His Son, never leaving, never forsaking,
    bringing me courage, bringing me peace.

O Lord of the morning, Lord of the night,
    Your Spirit's within me, helping me see.
It's You I would worship.
It's You I would praise.
Guide me this new day, now and always.

My Question to Harry

The calendar tells me sixteen years ago,
    my Brother,
you were taken through that Last Gate
    which leaves nothing unchanged.
If all is different, how can it be true,
    you are still yourself to me?

River, beside my window, are you the same
    as you were in years gone by?
Shimmering water reflects the same light,
    sapphire, amber, pewter, gold.
Yet small twists and shapes became different
    as the years moved past.

The sandy shore, now eroded,
    slopes toward the water.
Bright blossoms and springtime grass
    add new freshness to its banks.
Sea birds still skim the river's face
    watching for silvery glint of food.

The same, yet not. It's changed somehow.
Is this the way with you, my Brother?
In stillness the river's murmuring voice
    is an echo of your own,
"Yes, I am myself, the same you remember.
Yet all within this soul is new." *

*Amy Carmichael's poem, *The Question,* from her book.
Toward Jerusalem was my inspiration and pattern for this
poem.

The Ringing of Bells

Two children born four days and eight hundred
        miles apart, Bill in Mansfield, Ohio,
        Fran in Atlanta, Georgia.
It seems strange after sixty years of marriage
        that we moved from womb to college
        without knowing each other.
Two classes at Wheaton College introduced us,
        geology lab and Dr. Singer's History.

On a lovely fall day as I was painting on campus
        Bill walked by and said, "Hi."
I said, "Hi." He hurried off.
Twice more he passed, coming from the same direction
        and saying, "Hi."
Stopping on the third round, he asked me
        to go to a senior recital with him. I accepted.

We dated fairly regularly the rest of the school year.
I liked him, found him interesting,
        nice in every way.
With promises to write we went separate ways.
By summer's end we were writing every day,
        our thoughts, beliefs, hopes and plans.

At the time I didn't realize it but now I do.
We fell in love through our letters.
Love was not discussed in the letters
        but on occasion a whisper very close
        to love bled through the lines.

As the train pulled into Union Station Chicago
      I wondered if he would kiss me.
With great enthusiasm we threw our arms
      around each other.
He kissed me three times on the cheek
      as we laughed with joy.

A great orange moon climbed the darkness
      that night as we watched from our table
      by the silver edged Fox River.
It was on its banks he proposed as Mr. Moon
      smiled approvingly.
I said yes and he kissed me, a lovely,
      happy, tingly kiss. Sweet and strong.

Mother offered him her grandmother's diamond
      which he had the jeweler set in Tiffany style.
It was my Christmas present in 1948.
When Bill's buddies at school saw the big sparkler,
      they christened him the Zircon Kid.

Wheaton tradition for newly engaged couples
      is they climb the Tower's winding stairs
      at moonrise announcing their love
      by ringing the Tower bells.
Twenty-one joyful bongs and dongs encircle
      campus with glad tidings of joy.

February

A month still bruised by winter's grip
    is blue, gray and purple.
Skeleton trees, tall, lank shadows,
    sway to a minor key.

Wind pipes a note. Branches start to move,
    dancing with wild abandon.
A chill creeps in, lights dim.
A snow ballet begins.

Lacy flakes float down in full white skirts
    covering the cold scarred Earth.
Silence piles up in soft, muffled heaps,
    my thoughts a contrast to winter.

Day is icy and wind is sharp,
    but in my heart is a coal of joy.
It's glowing there by the Spirit's power
    no winter storm can chill.

Both Named Nash

There were two little children, both named Nash,
    Bill was six, Kakie was four.
Both were gifts from God's great plan
    to make up a family of four.

Their daddy traveled weekly
    while mother taught school.
When Daddy returned from his five day trip
    he brought each a Steif toy.

They had foxes and bears, kittens and ducks,
    tigers, wolves and buffalo.
In grown-up talk we call them friends.
The children called them "frins."

We made a Privacy Pact concerning our rooms,
    to help keep down the strife.
Other members may visit
    but by invitation only.

Bill spread his animals out on the floor
    and led them on grand adventures.
Kakie sat cross legged, as close as she dared,
    intrigued and barely breathing.

Emphatically reminding his sister of the Privacy Pact
    he drove her from the room.
She sat in the hall by his door taking care
    that no toe crossed the threshold.

Meanwhile seeking a peaceful solution
      while honoring the Pact,
I, the mother suggested we take Kakie's "frins"
      on a fine adventure.

Kakie's big blue eyes teared up.
      Her tender lip quivered.
Blurting out her difficult problem, she sobbed,
      "But Muver, my "frins" can't talk!"

My education commenced quickly.
      You Lord, let it be wisely.
My children, both named Nash, put me
      in a box more quickly than they
      put their "frins" away.

Most Things Change

My little children, both named Nash,
    have grown up now.
The tiny girl has become a woman,
    the little boy a stalwart man.

It seems strange, Lord, to look
    from memories, idealized a bit,
to three dimensional events of today,
    then squint through the foggy
    questions of tomorrow.

Most things in life change frequently
    and show no sign of stopping.
We started our family as two
    but soon we became four.

We four became six. Four of the six
    produced five more.
Two of the five found brides,
    bringing our number
    to thirteen.
One of the brides will soon produce
    another little child named Nash.

Squint as I may through the foggy future,
    the question of numbers
    will bring me no answer.
Another little boy becomes a man,
    a girl becomes a lovely woman,
    and numbers change again.

A Lap Full of Warm Puppy

Today I'm thinking how nicely a lap full of warm puppy
and cold New Jersey days compliment each other.
Scrappy Nash, a wondrous bit of creation, is ever alert,
awaiting my early morning quiet time.
It's her opportunity to sit on my lap, be my book rest
as our respective circulatory systems warm us.

Our bright eyed Scotty, whom I love and enjoy,
demonstrates spiritual lessons daily.
Her tongue tells no tales but her actions speak volumes.
By watching her I see expectation, hope, trust, obedience
and unconditional love in action every day.

Scrappy is a parable, not in a book, but in a black fur coat.
Lord, thank You for the gift of this small bit of life
and loyalty, and please, Lord, remind me to learn daily
from my humble little friend.

An Old Dandelion

A woman of age steps from the shop
     going to a ladies tea.
She's carefully dressed, carrying a cane
     of ebony, with silver crook.

Wrinkled cheeks glow with healthy blush,
     color straight from a box.
Beneath the eyes shadows lurk
     under their ivory mask.

Well shaped nails of rosy gloss
     tip her knotty fingers.
Hair so clean it shines silver in the light,
     clipped, combed, pampered, glued.

Mirror's image brings approving, "Aha!
Purse may be empty but pride stands tall!"
Parking the car at her destination
     the queen steps out well pleased.

Alas! Playful puffs of autumn breeze
     swirl the coif with a windy chuckle.
Window reflection shows no regal queen,
     only an old dandelion gone to seed.

"Pride goes before destruction, a haughty spirit before a fall."
Proverbs 16:18

All Creation Sings

Jesus, Savior, Eternal King, Lord of all I see,
    creation is praising You.
It finds no words yet I hear its music
    in sunshine, sky and tree
    and its melody captures my heart.
Jubilant flowers unfold before me,
    adding fragrance to the breeze.

Mountains, flowers and turbulent sea,
    I join my praise with yours.
Though He made you eons ago,
    and I am but mortal child,
His love has warmed my stony heart
    giving words to my song.

Come then, Creation, let's blend our praise,
    come angels, mortals and stars,
Let's sing praise in morning,
    at noon and again in velvety night.
Let it ring out now and forever more,
    our Holy God is eternally praised!

Appetite For God

While day is early, sweet and new,
I turn first thing to You.
Your blessings fall like freshening dew
upon my thirsty heart.

Lord, let me sing this song to You,
this song of love and praise.
I know Your Name, I see Your Hand
in all my eye takes in.

I begin to sense astonishing things,
things I never expected.
Good books I read three times or more,
that seems to be enough.

But as I drink Your Word
in gratifying gulps
I recognize my hearty
appetite for You.
Your Word satisfies perfectly
and yet I always want more.

Companion of the Way

This journey seems long
        and I am wearied some.
A gate called Necessity
        through which I must pass
        lies shrouded, dark and lonely.

Companion of the Way,
        our eyes meet, You ask,
"Do you forget so soon?
Have I ever left you to walk alone,
        failed to cheer, to see you through?"

 I stop, kneeling at Your feet, confessing
        with shamed yet joyful tears,
"Never, Lord, You are faithful
        even when I forget!
Forgive and restore my praise."

Taking a faith-filled breath,
        I step out in timid hope.
You lift me, refreshed, to Your path again.
Fear dissolves in remembered light
        shining on Your golden Way.

Innocent as Morning

Baby, little baby, sated with milk,
      lulled by sleep,
      who are you?
An unmarked slate, lying no lie,
      scheming no scheme.
Your needs so many, your replies so few,
      a cry or a smile will do.

Baby, baby from God's plan
      innocent as Eden's morning.
Soft and warm, a precious weight
      filling empty arms.
Your sleeping beauty stirs my heart,
      delicate lashes on flawless cheeks.

Small, downy head of undreamed potential
      trusts upon my shoulder.
Miniature hands, tinier fingers
      holding tight.
Translucent toes on kissable feet
      working from covers.

Sleep on tiny child, know that God
      loved and cared for you
as He knitted you together gene by gene
      and cell by cell.
Grow strong, return His love
      and learn to share it.

No Leash for Me

Summer is here. So is Auntie.
As we drive to the mountains
     I perch on her luggage
     'cause Peaches took my seat.
She's an unhappy dog,
     and lets it be known.
Uncle Jack sings as he drives,
     adding his bass to her yodel.
The duet brings out my giggles,
     behind my hand, of course.

Mother plans a picnic
     with swimsuits and towels.
Peaches the poodle is with us
     quivering on her leash.
It nearly turns me green
     to see her daintily sniffing
     night's droppings
     of fox and possum.

"No water wings for you, Francie.
Today you learn to swim,"
     Auntie says with determination.
"I'll just tie my rope around you
     to keep you sa --"
"Oh, no," I squeak,
     running for the river,
     "I'll not be like Peaches,
     a dog on a leash!"

I leap in the river with a splash and a gasp,
        a struggle and a thrash.
I swim six strokes, emerge huffing
        and puffing, wearing a smile.
"I can swim! I can swim!
No leash for me!"

Planning to Grumble

My family was out of town for several days.
None of the three remembered their promise
    to finish certain tasks.
Since I was having guests tomorrow
    I did the chores myself.

After ten hours, my back hurt. I was tired,
    dirty and resentful.
Making a quick sandwich, I took it outside
    to watch the sun set
    and commiserate with myself.

I planned to grumble to You, Lord,
    about poor ol' me.
But the beauty of the garden, late golden light
    through the trees
    jolted the ugliness from me.

With one surprised gasp I asked You to forgive me,
    to bless and protect my travelers.
I told You I missed You during my resentment,
    and thanked You for painting
Your glory across the sky in sunset colors.

Who else, Lord, would treat a grumpy,
    selfish woman the way you have,
    lavishing Your love on me tonight?
No one else, Lord. No one but You!

Birds at Nest

When light begins to close her eyes
    and night falls like a veil,
    my heart begins to tune her praise
    in Your restoring presence.

This off key day was in Your hand
    and now the night is Yours.
My loved ones scattered about the land
    are kept in Your own way.

Quiet joy and rest of soul settle in
    like birds at nest, for Lord,
Your forgiveness lifts my heart
    as day fades into night.

Quietness and peace, past understanding,
    enfold me in the joy of Your presence,
    lifting my soul on strong wings
from shadows into the light of Your love.

Lion and Lamb

The lion of March
    is on the prowl
    roaring through
    the skies.
He moans and cries,
    growls and sobs,
    expressing man's
    inner hunger.
At last he's weary,
    his fierce breath
    fading to
    gentle breeze.

The lamb steps in
    to welcome spring
    just around the corner.
Spring thaws the ground,
    renews the soul,
    drops down
    crystal showers.
Hearts are lifted,
    days grow brighter,
    sensing new life
    unfolding.

A Garment of Shining Light

Chariot of Fire, unseen, not heard,
    sweep through light years of space.
Transcend time which binds us here,
    pull in beside her bed.

She'll spring right up from her empty shell,
    leap in with joyous step.
Drive straight and true, O Angel of Death –
    through to Heaven's realm.

There in God's Kingdom she'll drop
    off the old and slip on the new
    like a garment of shining Light.
Daddy will be there, bright in glory,
    smiling with joy.

Together they'll sing a brand new song,
    like praise we've never heard.
So, Angel, swing low in a flash of an eye,
    come down for her tonight.

This prayer song came to me the night before my mother died in 1974. Now in 2008, as my only remaining sibling stands at the Last Gate, this prayer rises once again in my heart.

Are You With Me Now?

Lord, are You here with me now?
I see no footprints on today's path
    except my own.
Am I left to battle twin giants
    of Doubt and Fear alone?
I speak but do You listen? What did I do?

Perhaps, Lord, You are testing me, letting me
    know I can trust You even if You're silent.
When all is tranquil and I know You are close,
    why shouldn't I trust You?
If I think You are not here today am I not
    putting my thoughts above Your Word?

Your long remembered promises stir hope,
    "I will never leave you.
I am with you to the end. Friends may fail
    You but I will not.
Your name is forever engraved upon My Hands.

Even if your mother deserts you, I will not.
Look. I have engraved you on the palms
    of my hands."

This is a prophetic promise of God written by Isaiah seven
hundred years before Christ's birth. The engraving on His
hands was done by iron nails at His crucifixion. Isaiah 49:16

Big Papa's Pants

It's summer time in Atlanta 1929.
At Springdale the men folk gather on the verandah
    in late afternoon in shirt sleeves
    and start rocking chairs in slow motion.

The women join the men or gather separately
    to sip ice tea with a sprig of mint,
    moving palmetto fans back and forth,
    back and forth.

Big Papa, my grandfather, a sturdy, jolly man
    with rosy cheeks, blue eyes and white hair
    seems to enjoy my five year old
    childish antics.

When he sees me coming up the drive
    he waves his ever present fly swatter
    and calls, "Hello, Cutie!"
He never calls me Francie as others do.
I'm always Cutie.

Even in midsummer men wear suit coats
    except in the privacy of their homes.
Big Papa, Uncle Buddy and Uncle Frank always
    wear coats when they come to visit.
As Annie Mae answers their ring, she says,
"Evenin' Mr. Akers, come in. Let me take your coat."

Thursday is Annie Mae's day off.
The door bell rings on Thursday.
It's Big Papa. He's not wearing a coat!
Nothing daunted, I do my best in the absence
        of proper protocol.
I say, "Come right in Big Papa and take off your pants."

Big Papa's laugh is an extended roll
        of happy thunder while he wipes tears
        from his mirth filled eyes.
Big Papa did not remove his pants.

A Name Above all Names
A paraphrase of Psalm 8

David must be on his rooftop garden this starry night. He is
filled with awe not only at God's creative power but his
loving mercy toward fickle humanity.

> Jehovah-God! That Name above all names!
> It echoes through the halls of Creation
>   and overfills the heavens.
> Babies and toddlers lisp Your Name,
>   bringing their prayers to You.
> Surely, Lord, their trusting praise should
>   squelch pagan mockery.
>
> That night sky above me, Lord … huge! Enormous!
>   Overdoming the earth!
> Even its blackness is aflame with glory.
> Crowded stars brilliant moon. All burning.
> Shining. Praising. Magnifying Your power.
>
> It causes me to wonder, Lord, why You bother
>   with us earthlings.
> We are simply miniscule dots in the throbbing cosmos
>
> And yet You made us only a bit lower than angels.
> You honor us with Your love and crown us with
>   Your mercy. You visit us with forgiveness,
>   placing creation under our rule.

In Eden's morning we came so close to Your perfect
plan, and yet …

O Lord, our Lord, Your perfect Name thunders,
it whispers. It permeates the cosmos,
truly a Name above all names!

A Singing Soul

It's a Gothic cathedral,
    this forest of trees,
    overlaid with emerging green.

God's Presence is here,
    is almost seen in the beauty
    He has made.

Sunlight leaps
    from rain drenched leaves,
    like fingers flying over keys.

Music rises
    through each vaulted arch,
    an allegro of rousing joy.

He lives in me,
    this mighty God, as He creates
    a singing soul.

My joy rings out
    in buoyant praise
    to my Lord
    whose peace is here.

Lord, it's true! Songs seem to bubble up unbidden from some clear, cool spring deep within me. To see You in nature or to recognize Your living Presence in another of Your children invariably starts a song singing itself out in me. Psalm 40: 3

Who am I Today?

Lord, at times I wonder just who I am today.
Auto permit, passport and social security
        say I'm still old so-and-so.
More identifiable things are no longer here.
They have vanished.

My children are not children anymore.
They are adults with families of their own.
Health, strength, beauty and youth
        have left me without recognizable identity.
Social standing now sits on the back row.

Hosting, teaching, traveling widely
        are only picture albums lining my shelves.
Memory dims around the edges,
        so if I'm not who I used to be,
        then who on earth am I today?

I look around the house searching
        for a definable identity.
Surely I have one somewhere.
Can it be, because things are aching,
        I'm looking for my "now self"
        in all the wrong places?

Answer to Who am I Today?

Lord, sometimes when breathlessness takes away
    my speech, when limbs grow heavy
    and eyes dim down to a low burn.
When time hangs heavy, when old friends die
    and young friends rush past,
    I'm tempted to sag, to question my worth,
    my identity.

At times like this You remind me to look back,
    to remember numberless times
    You rescued me from fear and doubt.
I remember I am "fearfully and wonderfully made."
I remember other of Your astonishing words:
"I formed you in the womb, knew you before birth,
    set you aside as My very own."

Mighty God of time and eternity, this tells me
    I am rooted and grounded in You.
Roots hold my beginnings and endings together,
    bonding Your eternal identity to me
    which cannot be removed.
When all I do makes me think myself is gone
    I am still known, loved and redeemed
    by You, my Father in Heaven,
    from whom my confidence comes.
You are my Eternal Identity always and forever.

Beyond the Blue

Glory of morning, earth, sky and water,
        gems of new day, wake up and sing.
Transparent air, golden in light,
        images mirrored on sapphire sea.
Thoughts take wing, flying high, yet higher,
        raising questions causing me to wonder.
Has it entered my heart of clay
        what awaits me beyond the blue?

If this life is glory, if heaven is real,
        what of the City prepared for me?
What of New Jerusalem, bright jewel of Grace,
        anchored in Power, glowing with Life?

Fair City of Heaven, soon to be seen,
        has no earthly comparison,
        not Earth's mountains of strength,
        nor moon with her grace.

Dawn, you throbbing opal of beauty,
        merely a pale reflection
        of my Home beyond the blue.

Goodbye Santa

Christmas is near,
    just around the corner.
Santa will come soon
    my kindergarten friends say.
And strange things are happening here
    at home, making me wonder.

Packages arrive, then disappear
    without a word.
Conversations stop abruptly
    when I enter the room.
My curiosity demands
    a thorough investigation!

Mother's closet has always held
    a fascination for me.
Perhaps answers lie on those
    unreachable shelves.
But shelves are high, near the roof.
    I'm still small, close to the floor.

Hearing no sound, while holding
    my breath, I open the door.
There's a new big box poking out
    from shelf seven.
What could it be? Could it be
    something for me?

Not calculating risks I begin the climb.
If I move from shelf two up to three,
    why not from four to five?
Standing on six, holding to seven,
    I push the corner of the mystery box.
Beneath layers of tissue I see a white shoe
    on a doll's right foot.

On the way up the climb is exciting
    but looking down it's scary.
Here I am close to the ceiling,
    now how do I get down?
Shelf by shelf on groping feet
    I gain the floor undetected.

Tomorrow has come. It's Christmas Day.
    The tree twinkles in morning's new light.
Gloria is here in white shoes and socks.
    Understanding has dawned. Reality appears.
Hello, Gloria. Goodbye, Santa!

Pick Me Up Lord
A paraphrase of Psalm 143

Almighty God, hear my prayer! Listen to my words.
In Your faithfulness and mercy, answer me.
Don't judge me harshly, Lord, for no one is truly just.

You know how I feel. The enemy has knocked me down
      and pounded me into the ground.
I'm in total darkness as to what to do. I feel as though
      I'm already dead ... heavy and listless.
All courage has drained from me. I'm desolate.

I remember Your awesome deeds. I study Your works
      and am astounded. I hold up my arms to You.
Lord, pick me up! I thirst for You
      as crops thirst for rain.
Help me quickly! I'm dizzy and faint.
Reassure me and Your assurance will sustain me
      throughout the day.
I'm lifting my wide open soul to You. You are my God,
      so show me the way.

O Lord, resuscitate me for the sake of Your Name,
      for the sake of Your mercy and justice,
      bring me out of this crisis.
Overcome those who would destroy me
      for I belong to You.

Our Lifting Lord

When Bill and Kakie were small
        they reflected their remorse
        by downcast heads, flushed cheeks
        and brimming eyes.

I remember gathering the little repentant one
        on my lap, lifting the quivering chin
        and kissing away the tears.
You do that with us, Father. You comfort,
        restore, forgive and encourage us.

When we grown ups come to You
        as a little child
        admitting our guilt and weakness,
        asking for and accepting
        Your forgiveness and strength
        we are in a similar way
        gathered into Your lap
        and hugged.

You lift us from shame and dejection.
Your love shines out like light,
        chasing away the gloom.
"They looked to Him and He filled them
        with His Light.
Rather than reflecting their shame
        their faces glowed with His Light."
                                        Psalm 34:3-6

Good Morning, Lord

Good morning, Lord! Earth still sleeps.
    There's neither sound nor light.
Silent trees stand resting.
    May Jesus Christ be praised!

I'm lethargic, drugged with sleep,
    thoughts still dim and formless.
Darkness fades without a murmur,
    May Jesus Christ be praised!

Coffee pot chuckles. Birds wake up,
    morning looks in my window.
It softly starts the day's song,
    May Jesus Christ be praised!

I asked You, Lord, to wake me early
    so we may have our visit.
I'm singing now with trumpets of dawn,
    May Jesus Christ be praised!

Here I am, and here You are.
Gather me up and shape me to fit
    Your plans today.
May Jesus Christ be praised!

Locked In With Myself

Lord, I'm hungry for warm, fresh Bread,
    and thirsty to drink Your Living Water
    to flood my drying soul.

How did this happen? Why did I leave
    the place of greening growth
    to enter desert's barren scape?

Actions are unchanged. Time set aside
    for worship, door closed for quietness.
Holy Book lies open before me.

My soul asks, "What is this about a door,
    a *closed* door? Did I close the door
    to heart and mind, keeping You out?"

Peter saw Jesus crossing the water
    and his faith leaped high.
It failed him as he looked at the waves.
Like Peter, I saw only my fear, failing to see
    my Savior's extended hand of rescue.

Yes. I've locked myself in with anxiety.
No wonder hunger gnaws
    and lifting joy no longer lifts.
Forgive me, Lord. Will I ever learn?

Dark Clouds

Have you watched a summer's day darken
    as clouds sweep over the sky?

Have you listened to stillness as earth
    holds her breath before the storm breaks?

Have you smelled the fragrance
    of the first rain drops on crumbly dry soil?

Have you wondered why rain must come,
    ruining carefully laid plans?

Have you noticed what happens as grass
    and forest accept the rain?

Does grass refuse refreshing showers,
    do forests hold back new growth?

Lord, as the forest drinks in the rain may
    I accept disappointment in a positive way
    from Your loving hand.

April's Dawn

May God be praised in Heaven and Earth
    this shining April dawn.
Earth hears Your great command,
    "Rise up from winter's tomb!"
Trees respond with colorful cheer,
    twigs grow bright with sap.

Tiny creatures tune their fiddles
    as soon as darkness falls.
All nature sings in joyous rhythm
    with chirp, or croak, or whistle,
for winter's grip has lost its hold
    and life breaks free at last!

O that mankind would praise You so
    for all Your wondrous ways.
Our dark depths would heed Your call,
    "Turn to Me and live!"
Chains of night would fall away,
    and mankind would be reborn!

The Hunt Revisited

It's a golden morning, sky as blue
    as a sky can be.
Breeze sends shivers up the river,
    its banks are lacy with budding trees.

Hot air balloons, shaped like giant eggs,
    begin their ascent reminding me
    of Easter Sunday's egg hunt,
    with scampering feet and happy squeals
    accompanying each discovery.

Our yearly hunts are over all too soon
    for eager grandchildren.
Not true of the endless treasures
    Almighty God hid in earth, sky and water
    challenging us to discover.

Tucked away are minerals, jewels,
    chemicals and formulae.
He planted principles, truths, moral, natural
    and spiritual laws. God knows our joy
    in both the search and discovery.

Into space He flung planet sized "eggs,"
    invisible till darkness covers all else,
    leaving them to wink and shine.
We ask, "How can we reach that twinkle?
Who made it? Can we make use of it?"

That's, what You want, isn't it, Lord,
    to show us Yourself?
Your marvels always beckon us,
    showing us a bit
    of what You know.

When we discover that You indeed
    are the greatest treasure of all
    our hungry hearts are filled
    and our longing souls satisfied.

Kay

My sister, playmate, mentor and North Star,
    just stepped from time into eternity.
Though I'm glad her suffering is over
    there's a deep hole in my heart.

This was no casual sisterhood as some may have.
Our lives and hearts were intertwined.
As children we acted out adventures with homemade
    paper people from the Land of Inks.

In North Carolina mountains we rode Blackie
    bareback, two girls on one horse,
    crossing meadows and apple orchards,
    splashing through frisky streams.

Kay taught me to write my name, to enjoy books,
    to hope to write one some day.
Together we loved Amos, our dog, Billy, her canary,
    Beelzebub, the ally cat and Waddles my duck.

We marveled at budding trees, sprouting seed,
    and colors other than blue in evening's sky.
Daddy introduced us to God's solar system
    using his great telescope to illustrate.

As years took us separate ways from Atlanta
    fat newsy letters filled with joy
    and blessing kept us in touch as we discovered
    new signs of God's love.

In summers Kay rented a large beach house
    inviting her nephews and our Kakie.
Kakie, the only girl, was to be Kay's playmate
    and helper among seven noisy boys.

Memories built up summer after summer
    each leaving an impression.
Combined, they began shaping men from boys
    and women from girls.

Kay has left us, gone from this earth,
    but her fingerprints are on us.
She left us but her influence remains
    a bright part of us forever.

A Tightly Folded Tent

Stunned, I stand by the casket
  of my sister, a part of my heart.
There lies a fragile skeleton
  draped in near transparent skin.

It seems all that made Kay herself is gone,
  leaving an empty shell,
  a withered blossom,
  a tightly folded tent.

Saying goodbye I place my hands over hers.
Contrasts in our hands, hers waxy, lifeless,
  mine, warm and rosy with life's blood,
  tell the story.

Was she perfect? No …
  just perfectly human,
  endowed with numerous quirks
through which love, beyond self, flowed.

Is this empty shell, once busy and quick,
  cradling vibrant personality,
transformed by God's indwelling Spirit,
  all we have left of her? No.

She's home now, Lord, "with You in Paradise."
That comforts us, yet it leaves us lonely too.
Within us live memories of Kay
  with power to bless or hurt us.

52

Her influence still presses in on our lives,
    molding hearts and minds
    by the strength of her faith
    and unchangeable love.
Help us, Lord, to hold her memory
    and grow with it.

"Death walks through life holding the hand of each of us.
It eventually leads all to the grave with empty pockets. But as
for me, I have a Redeemer. He alone has the power over death.
And when His time is right, He will receive me into His holy
house forever …very much alive." *

* Paraphrase of Psalm Forty-nine from *Let All Creation Praise
Him,* Frances J. Nash, 2002

Love Knows The Way

Lord, I'm trying hard to pray
    a "sufficient prayer,"
a wise and efficient one
    to fill her need.
But I'm wordless … a blank
    before her young pain.

You love her yesterday, today
    and all her tomorrows.
In the powerful presence
    of Your faithfulness
my words are as inconsequential
    as my lack of ability.

Any prayer I make today rings
    hollow in my heart.
No sculpted prayer is needed,
    no wringing of hands.
Your Love knows the way to peace.
Your promise and my trust
    will lead her there.

While in a crisis, my prayers are mostly cries for help. It was in the writing of this I rediscovered, peace from fear and trust in God's faithfulness.

May Is …

May is morning
    dipped in coolness
    tender fresh.

May is fragrance
    breathing out
    intoxicating senses.

May is opal dawning
    from blackest night
    hung with stars.

May is crystal rain
    blessing earth
    bringing life.

May is promise
    from life's Creator
    of grace bestowed.

May is hallelujah!
    HALLELUJAH
    and Amen!

New Life Pictures

Joyful praise from hearts ascending
to our Lord who made this day.

Spring is born. All Nature sings it,
in color, growth and freshness.

Earth is drawing resurrection pictures
filling eyes with beauty.

Memories of amazing grace wake
my mind to hope anew.

Jesus! Jesus! Life's creator, flow through
me with signs of Spring.

Like the sap in leafless branches
You are shaping a fruitful tree.

Mold this flighty, stubborn will
till it becomes transformed.

Cause it to grow and have no Winter
because its roots are deep in You.

When My Time Ends

Chilling whispers ride the wind
        fanning the flames of fall
        in every leafy wood.
River sings its song to sun
        with overtures of glory.

Whose artistic touch is this
        painting afresh the sunset
        moving with unseen brush?
Wordless, it speaks
        in vivid images.

It glows in light, patterned by shadows
        on nut brown earth
        and mossy greens.
Sunlight slips through fingers
        enlightening things beyond.

What's the song? What does it whisper?
Why this unnamed hunger,
        this yearning pain and silent need?
I wait and watch expectantly,
        seeking an answer.

Is this nostalgic longing
        my human, earthly need
        to touch Your garment's hem?
Face to face, when my time ends,
        You take my hand to lift me up.
My pain is gone. I know even as I am known.

Window with a View

Down among the trees and hills
    earth seems very large.
Sky and cliffs stretch up so high
    from valleys remote and deep.
But up here, Lord, with plane's eye view,
    I see with different eyes.

Bright clouds drop shadows on the sea,
    waves are merely ripples.
Mountains thrust skyward but still can't reach
    the unattainable blue.
Down there a ship takes a luxurious trip
    with merriment, feasting and song.

Deep blue water, lacy white wake, clouds
    like glory in the sun.
From here the picture is all off kilter,
    how toy like it seems to be!
Beneath me is home, that minuscule globe,
    while above there's ceaseless space.

Endless space … a mystery I cannot fathom,
    but Your love reaching me,
holding me fast to Yourself, is the mightiest
    mystery of all.
You, Eternal, Infinite, spoke the Word
    and these worlds came to be.
Then Your love reached throughout vast
    expanse and claimed this finite me!

Presence of the Holy

Sleep refuses to answer my call,
        dark hours unwind slowly.
Why not desert the twisted covers,
        sit by the window
        and watch for morning?

Outside my tower it's black and still,
        no traffic sounds
        on road or river,
        no voice or shrilling phone.

Here in night's aloneness,
        wrapped in silence,
        clothed in awe,
        breathing seems an intrusion,
        restless time stands still.

There's only quietness and awareness
        of Your Presence,
        O Emmanuel. *
My whole being drops to her knees
        before Your blazing Holiness.

* *Emmanuel* means God With Us

Why Not Lord?

Yes, Lord, I understand that Your ways
    are not my ways, neither are
      Your thoughts like mine.
I know I was young once ... but not anymore.
I realize I'm an old woman ... but not for long.

Yet I'm in the dark as to why You programmed
    bodies to do such odd things.
Hair turns white, then falls out,
    but is it truly gone? No! It pops out
    on unsuspecting ears, chins or upper lips.

Some parts grow larger ... like noses, feet,
    bellies and big blue veins.
Eyes shrink, their lids like awnings
    while lips practically disappear.
Places which have no business hurting hurt ...
    hips, knees, back and fingers.

Memory dims and sun's glare blinds us.
Sleep is a shy visitor at night
    but during the day she is demanding.
The easy swing of walking leaves us
    and becomes tottering.

Noses run and feet smell. Why this peculiar
    turn of events?
Why not leave us strong, beautiful and healthy
    until You need us up There?
Why not, Lord? Why not?

Beyond Winter

Our lifetime usually consists of four seasons
    not unlike a year.
Life's springtime is our beginning. We are dependent,
    cherished and start our small life with parents.

Summer, our youth, is a time of growth and questions
    as we struggle for independence.
Autumn brings responsibility, success and failure,
    earning, gathering, influencing.

Last of all comes winter, our shortest season,
    a time to weigh life's lessons practiced,
    a chance to prepare for beyond winter.
Many things seem wrong in winter.

Our four cherished blessings, youth, strength,
    influence and beauty are either going or gone.
Try though we may with every current gimmick,
    we cannot reverse relentless seasons.

Lord, I believe You remove from us the trivia
    in which we take the most pride.
When it's gone we know no way to retrieve it.
We are more open to sit up and take notice
    of Who and what lies beyond our winter.
We concentrate on You.

My Man, My Husband, My Love

My man, my husband, my love,
    my heart warms yet to your touch.
Years upon years shared together
    bring understanding of things
    true, rich and lasting.
Young years, middle and old years
    mix in time's memory
    becoming "our life."

Circumstances change, we buy a house
    of stone and lumber, cold and silent,
    to shelter us.
In its sheltering it's warmed
    by the breath of our living,
    infused with our joy and sorrow,
    laughter and tears.

Both hearts and dwelling opened
    to Christ's call as He stood outside
    and knocked those decades ago.
As He entered through our faith,
    assurance and joy followed.

Babies, fruit of bodies joined in love
    grace our living with riches of kings.
Babies, in time, bring more babies to cycle
    outward, invading our gathering years
    with color and light
    breathing out joy and music.

My man, my husband, my love,
　　my heart is made strong
　　by your strength.
I am lifted by your constancy,
　　blessed by your faith.
Young years, middle years and old years
　　mix in time's memory
　　making a true celebration
　　of our long love.

To My Son on Father's Day

Son, my dear son,
    you are my love,
    my gift, my trust.
God honored and blessed me
    by sending you.

I loved you before I saw you
    face to face.
With that first sight,
    that first holding
    of your sweet warmth
    my love was sealed.
It is permanent from now
    throughout eternity.

Your caring and forgiving
    love for your children
    reflects our heavenly Father's
    love for us as we adults
    continue growing up.

You bless Dad and me daily
    with your faith, love
    and thoughtfulness.
Thank you for being you.

        I love you,
        Mother

My Grandson

This is the perfect way to celebrate Father's Day…
        by becoming one yourself.
Happy toasts! Congratulations!

Your wife is beautiful, daughter adorable,
        parents the best
        and grandparents … well,
        the four of us may seem a bit
        behind the times but we love you,
        enjoy your company
        and thank our generous
        Father in Heaven for the gift
        of you and your family.

                        Love,
                        Nannie and Papa

Autumn's Golden Touch

Cool crisp days of Fall's first month,
    sun that spotlights freshness.
Leaves choreographed to the Maker's tune,
    dance to the rhythm of change.

Silky waters, reflecting forests,
    sky as clear as tumblers.
Trees, shrubs and brawny poplar
    brighten to
Autumn's golden touch.

Crimson, blue, gold and winey-red,
    my mind recalls it well;
Earth's colors combine in brilliant praise
    as seasons broadcast His glory.

Small Tantrum

Earth hangs dimly beneath gray
    and darkening sky.
Rain approaches from far river bank,
    a ghost in diaphanous robes
    gliding ever nearer.

Hungrily devouring distance,
    and no longer silent, it attacks
    my unyielding windowpane
    with vicious persistence.

Wind-hurled drops against the glass
    distort my view of geraniums
    quivering red beneath the storm.
How awesome seems nature's small tantrum!

How comforting the windowpane between us!

Your Banner

Though wars rage fierce within my soul,
    Your Banner over me is Love.
Though questions rise and conflicts splinter,
    Your rallying Banner is Love.

Though trouble aims arrows, and tears
    dim my eyes,
when trembling Faith meets towering Doubt,
    Your Banner over me is Love.

Days move on, years multiply,
    yet Your covering Banner is Love.
In valleys dark it's there to see,
    Your bright Banner of Love.

If morning's wings could take me far,
    I'd see Your Banner there.
There's no place too distant, too low, too high.
    Your Banner over me is Love.

The Sure Foundation

Lord, You are my steadfast Rock.
Immovable. Secure.
You are the base to build upon,
        the one Foundation sure.

Age upon age comes and goes
        but You remain the same.
Nations ebb and flow as tides,
        heedless of Your Name.
But You are here, the very One
        who spoke worlds into being.

Seasons turn as kingdoms fall
        on Your catalyst called *Time.*
Men may curse You. Men may praise;
        both die with their decision.

Oh, Changeless God, may I realize,
        frail though I am,
 with You as my foundation,
        no wind can fell,
 or waters flood, the life built on You.

Ruthless Time

Ruthless Time taps out
    its rhythmic arithmetic.
Tiny seconds add up
    becoming minutes.

Mounting minutes multiply
    into hours.
Time subtracts from future
    while adding to past.

The sum of three months
    becomes a season.
Four seasons equal a year.
Years melt into a lifetime.

A present equation waits
    to be reckoned.
How to divide future's remainder
    by unfinished tasks?
Lord, multiply my strength to equal
    my remainder of days.

"Even when I am old and gray do not forsake me, O God, until I declare Your power to the next generation and Your might to all who are to come." Psalm 71:18

Today's Needs

Lord of grace, I seek You here
        among the chores of this day's needs.
I ask to walk these hours through
        and not to faint along the way.
I seek to run to do Your will
        and not grow weary with the task.

Wings of eagles lift me up
        as I await Your time.
By Your Spirit I sense Your strength,
        and spread my wings in Jesus' Name.
You are to me all joy and truth,
        the sound of music strong
        with peace.

I hail You now, my Lord and King,
        my true Companion
        in this day's needs.
Joyful praise lifts burdens
Whether they are physical,
        mental or spiritual.

Lacy White Petticoats

Fatigue unravels me. I must rest
    awhile beside the River.
It revives each chamber of my being,
    body, mind and spirit.
Today wind is strong, whistling,
    keening and sobbing,
    setting everything pliable in motion.

Sea birds catch wind's contagious exuberance.
Grace and strength accompany them
    as they swoop, hover, plummet and climb
    defying wind to disrupt their ballet.
Sun spotlights their feathered costumes
    transforming them into free spirits
    unencumbered by material flesh.

Earth's heartbeat continues thrumming
    in a rhythm all its own.
As wind lifts water, his graceful partner,
    he turns her in a lively reel.
She dances with vigor,
    her lacy, white petticoats
    flashing atop each wave,
    forming bright couplets on the water
    as far as the eye can see.

Rested, revived, enlivened I am buoyed
    by strong waves of God's peace.

What Have You Gained?

Lord, I see You in light of dawn
        as it sets day's clouds afire,
        over city, forest and river.
I see You in ancient oak, lifting
        mighty arms as in prayer,
        in wild flowers of the forest,
        bright colors from Your palette.
You ask me, "If you are not transformed
        by this what have you gained?"

I hear Your call in wind's melody,
        of breeze blown whispers,
        in carefree chuckle of brook leaping
        over smooth brown stones.
You speak my name in howling storm
        and crashing thunder.
Yes, I hear You in silence of starry nights
        blessed by peace and quietness.
Again Your query, "If you do not answer
        My call, what have you gained?"

Lord, I recognize Your hand
        in earth, sky and water,
        in midst of life's troubling pains
        of body and soul,
        in shadows of sorrow
        and uplifting brilliance of joy.

Yet again I hear, "If you are not made holy
by recognition of My power just what
do you think you have gained?"

We Give Thee Praise

We give Thee praise, our Father, for this world's beauty,
    for hours of our lives to worship Thee.
We praise Thee for the gift of forests and hills,
    for shimmering blue lakes
    and breeze blown trees,
    for wildflowers dotting woods with color,
    for the marvel of birds on the wing,
    for sunshine, shadow and fragrant days.

We praise Thee, Lord God, for Thy saving grace,
    for being the Water of Life within dry souls,
    for daily nourishment of Bread
    that is always fresh.

Praise to Thee, Jehovah-Jesus, for joy of companions,
    quiet blessings of contemplation,
    the guidance of Thy Word,
    for lifting songs, dance and merry laughter.

We praise Thee, Spirit of God, who seeks what was lost
    and draws it to its eternal home.
We rejoice in Thee for the assurance of peace,
    for the indwelling of Thy Presence.
Praise to Thee, Holy Three, Holy One,
    for Thy all encompassing Self within us,
    surrounding us, above us and among us.

In Celtic tradition

Once Upon a Day

Once upon a day I knelt beside my bed,
 knelt right down to pray,
 knelt to ask if God would help me.

In tears I told Him many things,
 of my selfishness and pain.
Told Him of my thirsty soul,
 told Him I needed Bread.

Waiting there I held my breath,
 to see if He could love me,
 to find out if He cared,
 wanting Him to be my Lord.

In stillness then I heard Him knock
 like the beating of my heart,
 like the patient call of One
 who awaits an invitation.

My eager hands unlocked the door.
In hope I flung it wide, wanting to see Him
 standing there,
 waiting to come inside.

There He was, like Heaven's Light,
 like Hope after despair!
He stood a moment with radiant smile,
 stood and then came in.

He wrapped me in eternal Love
        and said forgiveness was free.
He took me up in creative hands,
        began pressing out a shape.
Clay began to change its form
        reflecting the One who knocked.

I Wonder

I stand tonight under a great tree, wrapped in wonder,
    looking upward.
Moon's rays shoot like shining spears past giant limbs
    and rustling leaves, dropping pools of light
    at my feet.

The vision enters my eye, and moves deeper.
Breathing slows, racing heart is calmed.
Moving yet deeper, it whispers a hush over
    clamoring thoughts,
travels the depths of self and wraps
    the soul in peace.

Centuries ago a polished brown nut fell to earth
    to rest awhile.
Seasons shift, roots push down clutching soil.
Small bright flags unfurl in light announcing,
    "An oak is born!"

Today, Great Oak, you stand tall, deeply rooted,
    gloriously green, stretching skyward.
Drink your fill of sunshine and rain, paint cool
    shadows on hot summer ground.

I wonder. Is your purpose deeper than we humans
    often see?
Is there a message in your awesome beauty,
    in your strong endurance?
My soul answers, "Yes. You point to things beyond."

You are a beckoning, a flag waving, a signpost
        directing us to call our Creator,
a beautifully embossed invitation to us to go
        to Him in trust,
reminding us of Jesus' words, "Yes, I am here with you
        always, even until the end of the world."

Surrounded by Love

The green and gold scene in morning's new light
    looks in the window at me
and I look back with wondering eyes
    to watch You unfold the day.

Your Presence is here in rustling high leaves
    as well as the forest's depths.
What it says to me, Lord, makes my heart leap up
    with assurance of Your love.

Your love surrounds me, I know;
    it's deep in the future unknown.
Behind me it's there, like comforting years,
    solid beneath my feet.

I lift praise for Your love, and thanks
    to my King.
Here's worship with love returned,
    for I revel in seeing Your work.
So work, dear Lord, in the inner me
    and create a loving heart.

Mountains Still Sleep

Silent mountains still sleep,
　　dark giants resting.
Cradle moon hangs in western sky,
　　edging rough shoulders in silver.
Trees whisper quietly together
　　swaying in gentle dance.

Silence is pierced by clear birdsong,
　　trumpeting the finish of night.
Neighboring birds awake
　　joining the hymn of morning.

Timid light bleeds through blackness,
　　as the anthem swells.
Light intensifies, tingling with color,
　　brightening sky to coral flame.
Deep purple clouds slash
　　the glowing heavens.

Music, color, light and shadow proclaim
　　day's birth with riotous joy.
It makes me wonder, Lord, if You paint
　　ordinary days in this glory,
how can the Day of Your Return surpass
　　the splendor of this?

September's Song

Let heavens rejoice and earth be glad,
    let dawning laugh with joy!
May day break forth in endless praise
    and darkness shine as light.
For God's own world is singing His song,
    listen to earth's hymn of delight!

A song of growth, of rhythm and change,
    drenched in the fragrance of fall!
It rises with heat, descends with rain,
    sweeps over us on windy wings.
Earth's sights are a paean of praise to God,
    each ocean, each forest, each leaf.

O, that *we* would praise You so,
    with hearts to understand
    the wonders of transforming Love!
Lives would be mended, families made new,
    dark cities would ring with song.

Lord, kindle Your flame in hesitant souls,
    so Light drives darkness away.
Call us by name. Encourage us
    to step out and follow You.
Flood us in godly praise till we glow
    like this September's day.

The Quiet of Evening

I walked and talked through the coolness tonight
     with God the Almighty King.
I poured out praise in my weariness, He filled me
     with joy and strength.
I heard His words when day was done,
     His music lifted my soul.

There's nothing more blessed than an evening walk
     with the powerful Lord of all --
unless, perhaps, it's our morning visit
     while day is tender-soft.
Or might it be in afternoon as heat
     and pressures rise?

I need not choose between the hours
     for all day's hours are His.
But when dusk drifts down
     and day's deeds are done,
I seek His companionship then,
     to know the mercy in quiet of evening,
     of Jesus my Omnipotent Lord.

Three Way Love

I. *The Father's Love*

The Father's Love! No words can tell,
    no tongue describe its worth.
It lived before all Time began,
    remains when Time is gone.
The Father's Love! The mind can't grasp
    its height, its depth or breadth.
He spoke, and man became a living soul
    to multiply and spread.
He offered Love, unbound and free,
    for human kind to see.
But man was blind through unbelief.
    He didn't understand.
The love of God broke through the wall
    of darkened human hearts.
He put on the robe of human flesh;
    His Love sent Jesus here.

II. *Christ's Gift*

The Father's Love, who can know it
    in all its gracious care?
God is Spirit and we can not grasp
    the concept of Spirit alone.
So Jesus came, through humble birth,
    in order that we might see
Spirit and Flesh in dimensional form,
    pressed out and standing free.
He walked the path our feet should go,
    He demonstrated and explained.

He walked straight into death's dark jaws,
     walked through, then out again.
God's Love brought Him to us.
His Love took Him back, our Prophet
     and Priest and King.
As He entered anew into Heaven's realm
     His Love sent the Spirit of Power.

III. *The Spirit's Search*
     Seven fold Spirit, what love You show
          as You baptize with fire!
     Jesus is returning, but You walk now
          along the halls of earth,
     seeking temples not built by hands
          but living bodies of flesh.
     Your Love calls out to hungry hearts,
          "I've come to join your life!"
     So Spirit, come! My temple is crude,
          walls are buckled and cracked.
     Damp, shadowy places need Your Light
          to banish their moldy growth.
     Rebuild, transform me with Your Plan
          and pour out Your Love through me.
                  Amen

Wraparound Presence

Jesus said, "Be sure of this, I am always with you, even
to the end of time." (Matthew 28:20)

I praise You, Lord, Your wraparound Presence
        is always with me.
You are true Light, illuminating the dim soul.

Your love warms me and puts today's events
        into the perspective of eternity
rather than plunging them into coldness
        of enmity or hurt feelings.

Your forgiveness generates forgiveness in me.
Your Presence is fresh Bread, bringing
        nourishment for today's needs.

You are joy and strength, lifting me
        from the swamp of gloom.
Yes, Lord, my soul sings when I'm wrapped
        round in Your enlivening Presence.

October's Glory

Cornfields rustle, pale and crisp, a drawing card
    for crows wheeling against blue.
Landed, as bits of midnight, they strut
    their iridescent blackness.

Wind snatches color from ground and trees,
    twirling leaves across the roadway.
Undulating willows, in gold hula skirts,
    dance to the river's song.

Coppery pumpkins rest like fat eunuchs
    amid the clutter,
    while sun gilded squirrels
    scamper on fence and limb.

Such unique beauty for eye, ear and soul,
    and yet so fleeting!
October's fiery blaze fades too soon,
    extinguished by winter's silent white.

Don't be Afraid

It is dark. I am small, alone and frightened,
    covers clutched beneath my chin.
Black, twisty shadows creep closer ...
    noiselessly closer to my bed.
Suddenly the angel is there, filling the room
    with light of himself.

He does not resemble pictures of angels
    in my Bible story book
    of blond ladies in white bathrobes,
    with chicken feather wings.
Even with indescribable differences
    I know he is an angel.

He seems to consist of transcendent power
    and radiant light.
There is a sense of super human mobility ...
    more than any wings can supply.
His hair is like spun glass, amber in color,
    eyes glow from a strong, kind face.

Never having seen such a being, I am more
    startled than by spooky goblins.
Mother comes at my scream and turns on
    the sixty watt lamp.
The angel and his brilliance vanish, leaving
    the room in comparative twilight.

Remembering the experience, I ask myself
　　why he came, leaving no message.
Perhaps my Heavenly Father wanted to tell
　　this frightened little child
　　what He told others through the ages,
"Don't be afraid, for I am here with You."

Work Out What God Works In

Within my heart, Lord, I pray
    for a faith which endures,
    trust stronger than doubt,
    and unwavering loyalty.

Fear can slip in unannounced,
    grabbing center stage,
    turning off the light switch
    to hide God's truth in darkness.

Lord, You worked salvation into me,
    gave it freely with Your love.
Now, I need You to help me work it out
    as practical everyday relationships.

Isn't this the perfect way given us
    to show You to others? I think so.
May I reflect Your life in me as a tiny
    mirror showing a bit of Your truth.

Philippians 2:12

Learning To Mend

Here I sit, poised to grumble. I'm tired
    and want to go home.
Eyes burn from long days of reading,
    fingers cramped by writing.
Bottom's so numb it can't be mine!
Lord, mending bones takes patience.

Mind's just like a boiling pot
    of grumbles, sighs and wishes.
There are other places I'd like to be,
    jobs I could accomplish if only …
    if only, my feet would work
    without these clumsy crutches.
But I'm told, "Mending bones takes time."

So here I sit, growing wider, thinking,
    hoping, praying. Sit beside me,
    Lord of Healing,
    cool my heated fidgets.
Let these days somehow ripen my still green
    fruit called *Patience*.
O Lord! Mending bones takes
    so much time!

"Trouble brings patience, patience brings experience, and experience brings hope, and hope is not disappointing." (Romans 5:3)

Lord, use this time to work patience in me. I'll try to cooperate.

I'll Always Be Your Mommy

An illustrated child's book came
        with yesterday's mail.
Being many decades beyond childhood
        it surprised me by its arrival.

Pictured is a young mother rocking her infant
        and singing her love,
"I love you forever and I'll always
        be your Mommy."

Their years multiply, as years always do,
        but change never ceases.
Her baby grows into a little boy
        and moves to careless teens.

Illustrations show her, an awkward
        adolescent asleep in her lap,
        singing "I love you and will always
        be your Mommy."

He grows up as she grows old.
Age and frailty claim her.
Roles reversed, he lifts her to his lap,
        singing his reciprocal love,
"I love you and you will always
        be my Mommy."

The last illustration shows no mommy,
    but a big man, the son, rocking
    his infant daughter while singing,
 "I love you and I will always
    be your Daddy."

 A simple little tale of love's endurance
    moving through generations
    stirs my gathering memories
    deep and true.

They are not only of past days
    of rocking and loving
    but of my children's care of me
    in our reversed roles.
I know the joy of their strong, tender care,
    which brings tears, standing in my eyes …
    just waiting to fall.

Rocking on a Summer's Evening

Memories, decades old, leap vividly from past
        to present as similar scenes are visited.
Yesterday's years and today's ride together
        on life's merry-go-round
        in the blessed mystery of memory.

There they sit, the three of them on the porch
        rocking, talking quietly on a summer's evening.
I taste their peace, and remember rockers
        of another time moving in tandem.

Son Bill is there with our Kakie
        holding tiny Laurie Frances,
        her small downy head resting
        trustingly on Kakie's shoulder.
 The scene shifts back to another Bill and me
        on the porch at Springdale's Little House.

Late afternoon sun highlights masses
        of climbing roses and blue iris.
Ripe peaches, edible ornaments, glow from the tree
        just beyond the trellis.
A breeze redolent with summer perfume cools us.

Our baby, now a man, sleeps peacefully
        on my shoulder as Bill and I talk
        of our young dreams while evening
        lowers her lavender veil over another day.
Yesterday and today come together
        in a resounding, "Yes! I've been here before!"

Shadowed Blessing

Last night I was restless,
        lost in a fearsome valley of shadows.
Sleep scoffed my invitation to come
        stay the night as the third hip
        replacement loomed closer.
What if it doesn't work this time either?
Where is my faith? I could find it nowhere.

Groaning I see the clock indicates
        it's several hours till dawn.
Light filters through the shutters
        creating patterns on the ceiling.
Blinking, I look again at what I think I see.
It's the shadow of an angel with wings
        spread above my bed.

This can't be an angel's shadow!
Angels don't make shadows;
        they are not material beings.
But it may as well be an angel's shadow
        for it brings me blessing and peace.
Fretfulness seeps out, leaving room
        for my lost faith to return.

The lamp by my bed interrupting
        the passage of light makes
        the shadow angel, reminding me,
"He will give His angels charge over you
        guarding you in all your ways"…Psalm 91

In the Boat With You

Lord, amid slashing waves
    and shrilling wind,
Worn from press and needs of crowds
    You sleep upon a pillow.

Others row, till muscles tremble.
You wake to their cry, "Lord!
    We perish!
    Do You not care?"

You stand and speak to roiling sea,
    words You often speak to me,
    "Peace. Be still."
At Your command sea falls quiet,
    winds abate.

"Storms brew on every sea, in every life
    with power to destroy.
You need not fear. You will come through
    when I am in the boat with you."

Look Above the Storm
A paraphrase of Psalm 29

David's country is swept by war. He seems to be watching a
storm rage about him as he writes this prayer. Remembering
God's power calms him. The storm is frightening but he revels
in God's rule over all things, both in war and hurricanes.

All you strong sons and daughters give thanks to God.
Worship Him with awe in the presence of His might.
His voice thunders across the waters. Its sound enrages
     the sea. Majesty and power is heard in crashing waves.
Earth's inhabitants tremble before God's fierce symphony.

Your voice sweeps over the Land, O God.
A mighty storm splinters the great cedars of Lebanon,
     shaking them as they bow low in worship.
Lightning splits clouds, hurling fire to earth
     in forked brilliance.
The sound of Your voice explodes across the desert,
     stripping the wilderness.

Your decree brings life or death deep in the forest.
Both ruler and pauper quake as they marvel at Your power.
Yes, Lord, You still reign above this deluge of trouble.
You are King of all kings forever.
Bring Your people their needed strength and one day
     You will bring peace to Your Land.

Moonrise in November

I watch the river late at night,
    a black abyss beneath me.
I wait and breathe, see and sense,
    the quiet of aloneness.
Your swift moon races clouds,
    outlining them in silver.

It spreads a highway of light
    across the waters
    from its lunar face
    to these icy feet.
Cold air pierces summer's robe,
    teeth chatter from chill.
Yet the scene is mesmerizing,
    blackness and brilliance,
    midnight and gold.

Light cobbled roadway beckons
    where human feet can't follow.
Only mind and spirit are free
    to answer its summons.
Its beauty is God's call, reminding me
    of His power and glory.
It's in the joy of remembering
    my heart lifts in praise.

Wrapping My View in Glory

Lord, it's early. I'm too groggy to pray.
It's still dark as if day and I both
        have a problem waking up.
I'll just sit and watch You paint the morning.

Timid light is brightening more rapidly
        than my pen can write, reminiscent
        of flower films changing from bud
        to full blossom in a moment.

Coral, gold, pink and crimson flame out,
        staining the clouds with fire.
Your "strong man," the sun, is off like a shot
        running the race of day.

Color and light fall like music on dark waters.
River and sky, antiphonal choirs, take their part.
Sky drops its brilliance. River throws it back,
        wrapping all between in glory.

I'm awake now, Lord,
        for who could remain leaden
        in such a scene?

Wake Up My Soul
A paraphrase of Psalm 104

Wake up, my soul. I want to praise You, Lord.
But neither tongue nor pen can tell
    of Your greatness.
You cover earth with Your splendor,
    drenching it in light,
        drawing glittering heavens about it
        as a veil, dropping rivers and seas
        into her desolate places.

Clouds could be Your chariots
    as You ride on wings of wind.
You made angels as your messengers,
    bright and quick as flames.
This world, secure in space, was made
    and is sustained
    by Your laws of wisdom.

You flooded it, covering mountains
    with waters.
At Your command it took shape,
    waters found their assigned places.
Mountains pushed upward,
    valleys sank low.

You added springs in the valleys
    and wove streams through the land.
Birds live among the trees,
    filling the branches with music.

To high mountains You give water sources
  and earth is sustained by Your hand.
You breathe life into grass and grain
  to feed Your creatures.

Grapes yield wine to lighten man's heart
  from his burden of work.
His face glows with health and gladness.
Trees drink their fill of life giving water.
You populate rugged mountains with
  goats and badgers who build homes
  among the rocks.

I praise You for wonders of the moon,
  created as earth's glowing calendar,
  for sun, warming us, marking a new day.
As night falls beasts come out to find food.
Dawn breaks, they amble off to their dens
  and humans come out to earn a living
  until fading light drives them homeward.

Lord, Creator God, what You have made
  staggers the imagination.
Each creature, each star, every provision is made
  as a clear sign post pointing directly
  to Your caring power and merciful love.
Wake up, my soul, and look around you
  at God's handiwork.
Soak up the beauty! Pour out the praise!

Opening the Heart to Beauty

If God's creation of forest and river,
   sunset sky and greening earth
   does not infuse me
   with poems of praise
   what will?

Profusion of light and shadow,
   contrasts of fragility and ferocity,
   color and scent, jar trivia from me
   replacing it with amazed awe,
   snatching me from the sameness
   of my unseeing daily grind.

Standing beside the river reflecting
   golden dawn or fiery sunset
   rejoices my heart, freeing my soul
to soar and swoop as sea birds
   seeking a silvery meal.

Body, soul and mind are lifted,
   breathing in courage, trust, anticipation.
I turn from flavorless blandness
   toward blessing and peace
   opening my heart to beauty.

Your Bright Touch

Your touch shines bright in ambered fall,
    in early ending days.
Each tree claps hands of differing hue,
    each berry bright with life.

Crimson vine clings to gnarled old oak
    while bluets dance with the breeze.
Goldenrod claims the green hill's slope,
    and clouds billow overhead.

Eyes are drawn to surrounding hills
    cutting scallops in the sky.
Distant and cool in purple gauze
    they ring round fall's blaze.

Melodies of sounds and sights blend
    in a hymn of praise,
praise to the One who made all this
    for the children of earth to decode. *

*Decode, to convert into intelligible language, or to fit with the above usage: to look at God's creation and to ask ourselves, 'How did all this happen?   Who is behind it?   What is all this beauty telling me?   What does it mean to me as one person among billions?'

Pink, White, Blue and Gold

Our Kakie is a gift from the Giver of good gifts.
Mine was love *before* first sight of this baby
    with her wide blue eyes
    above cheeks as bright as sunrise.

Powerful potential for good and blessing
    lay in my arms that long ago day.
Cheerful optimism fills her small self.
There's also a streak of independence.

Early in the pabulum-applesauce stage
    she grabs wildly for the spoon
    saying persistently,
"Me feed it! Me feed it!"

Her grandmother taught her the desired reply
    to the question: "Kakie, what color are you?"
"I pink, whi', boo an' gole,"
    she proclaims with dimpled pride.
And so she was … pink and white skin,
    sky blue eyes and downy golden hair.

Years work their alchemy, the small bud unfolds
    as a lovely woman who is still
    pink, white, blue and gold.
Music, and the ability to make it,
    flows from this child of my heart,
    as I listen in astonished thanksgiving.

As sweetheart and wife of her husband
  she becomes a mother herself
  of three tall, handsome sons,
  strong and loyal Believers.

Decades slip almost unnoticed
  from past to present.
Today's scene finds me the needy one
  and she the guide.
Her tenderness, wisdom, loving consideration
  flows over and through me
  refilling me with astonished thanksgiving.

No Earthly Clue?

The manger where they laid You
        is crumbled and gone.
Your cross has turned back to dust.

Seamless robe, Your Mother's gift,
        has left no earthly clue.
Yet truth remains vivid
        in believing hearts.

You came, tender in baby flesh,
        pushed from woman's womb,
        came, in full surrender,
        completing the Father's Plan.

Millennia have passed …
        why consider it now
        when custom and pleasures call?

Father, crowd earth with Your angels
        flaming about unseen.
Renew and ignite us, O Lord,
        with knowledge of the Holy.

Send Your Spirit as mighty wind,
        while we simmer in our sin.
Remind us anew, King of Time and Eternity,
        why You gave us the Gift of your birthday.

Strange, Isn't It?

Strange, isn't it, how small events from past days
    imprint our lives, remaining for decades
    as if carved in stone?
I see a first grader, who is myself, upset over some
    trivial thing and advertising it
    by pouting face and angry comments.

Mother gathers me on her lap, smoothes my hair
    from hot, flushed cheeks and asks,
"What has distressed you, Francie?"
Not able to pin the blame on another, I hesitate,
    "I, uh, well … nothing really. I guess I'm just mad."
    "At whom are you mad?" she asks.

My lip trembles, tears fall amid a sob or two,
    "Nothing has gone right today! Jerry can't play!
    Anita is sick! I lost my …"

Mother quietly interrupts my tirade,
    "That's no reason to pour your bad humor
    over those not involved, is it? Yours are tears
    of self pity. You must stop immediately.
    If you find you cannot stop whining I will
    be obliged to give you a reason to cry."

I understand perfectly. With grubby little fists I dry
    my eyes, slip quickly from her lap, murmuring,
    "Yes, ma'am."

A moment later I'm on the floor happily playing Inks
    with my sister, Kay.
All thoughts of poor me are gone.
Thank God for strong mothers who direct
    their children with love and wisdom.

River's Bounty

It's an hour past midnight …
    dark as pitch outside.
A seven watt night light
    guides me to the window.
Looking down at the river
    with stars reflected on its surface
    and human activity beside it
I am reminded shrimping season is here.

All along the bank clusters of fisher folk
    gather round Coleman lanterns
    revealing spread blankets,
    bright shirts and ice chests.
Large round nets are flung high,
    unfurling as they rise
    like giant spider webs
illuminated against the darkness

Strong bodies cast and pull, bend and rise
    with the easy grace of dancers.
Shrimpers haul in their nets
    sometimes to disappointment,
    sometimes to pleasure of gain …
but always with hope of rejoicing
    in the river's bounty.

Remembering Mr. Twitchell

Mr. Twitchell, an unforgettable character
    from my childhood,
    lived in a one pump filling station
    down the mountain
    from our North Carolina property.

In summer the Johnston-Akers tribes gathered,
    each family in its own cabin.
All seven cousins liked Mr. Twitchell.
He often calmed troubled waters between
    teens and sometimes irate parents.

I, the youngest, was not generally included
    in their daring antics.
To me Mr. Twitchell was a dear friend.
He told me stories of mountain heroes
    and let me play with Cur, his shaggy dog.

Mr. T. was a skinny mountaineer, who from a side view
    formed a perfect question mark...
    in his tattered, almost blue bib overalls
    tired brogans with broken laces
    and shapeless felt hat with two "air holes."

He had a more salt than pepper mustache,
    which often disclosed the kind of soup
    he had for lunch.
Each Sunday he scraped the stubble from his cheeks,
    put on his tie and took off his hat.

Wrinkles, surrounding blue eyes, marked the abundance
of both his laughter and crushing pain.
Yes, it's a sweet yet sad interlude, on this stormy day
to remember an old impoverished mountain man
who helped build bright memories for seven
citified young cousins from Atlanta.

"Best Damndest Dam I Ever Seen"

Secretly the boy cousins decide to dam up
        the brook in the meadow,
            dreaming of a swimming hole nearby.
They tell their plan to Mr. Twitchell
        because they need his shovel.

When Cannie calls us to dinner
        the boys aren't back yet. We wait.
Mother, Auntee and Big Mama begin to worry,
        speculating on "what ifs."
Soon we see them trudging up the road
        with Mr. Twitchell.

With assurance of the boys safety, parental worry
        becomes anger. Explanations are demanded.

        "We built a great dam across the brook!
        It took longer than we exp …."

        "You're way overdue! Dinner is cold!
        Where have you been?"

        "I just told you. We built …uh … you
        tell 'em, Mr. T."

With the battered old hat crushed against his chest,
Mr. T.wants to help the boys in their hour of need.
"Well, ma'am, it's a fine dam. I never seen a better'n.
 It's jest the best damndest dam I ever seen
        crossin' over a crick!"

Dead Silence. Boys cringe. Parents stiffen.
Mr. Twitchell's smile melts in confusion.

After what seems an age, Mother responds
      kindly with understanding,
"Thank you, Mr. Twitchell, for supervising our boys,
      however we are unaccustomed to your words."
I hear smothered giggles as grimy hands
      try to quiet laughter's escape.

The boys earnestly hope and sincerely believe
      Mr. T's wicked word will defuse parental wrath.
Still clutching his hat to his heart,
      Mr. Twitchell turns to go
      when he hears Mother say,
"If you wait a moment, Mr. Twitchell, I'll have Cannie
      send a chicken dinner and apple pie with you."

Mr. T's old crinkly smile returns along with
      the twinkle in his eyes.
He realizes he is not excommunicated
      from the folks up the hill,
      he is only asked to watch his words.

The Gift of Choice

God gives His creation good gifts.
Hop toads hop, white ducks quack.
Birds sing, fly and swoop.
Elephants trumpet. Lions roar.

Dogs bark and wag their tails.
Cats climb trees and purr soft songs.
Pigs manufacture pork chops from table scraps.
Bored cows change grass to creamy milk
    with only one comment, "Moo-o."

God gives humans more gifts
    than we recognize,
        even more than we can name.
Among them is the gift of choice,
    something animals aren't given.

I may love or hate, I may help or hurt,
    bring peace or stir up trouble.
Will I choose to be generous or stingy,
    forgiving or resentful?
Will I allow myself to become a liar
    or choose to be a reliable person?

The choice is mine, no one can force me.
God will help if I choose His way
    and seek His guidance.
With His help that's what I want to do.

It's Summer Time

It's summer time, Lord, a season You are making
　　　day by day.
A picture comes to mind of a sunny afternoon,
　　　a hammock slung between shady trees,
　　　a resting woman watches wind form
　　　cloud pictures in the sky.
She hums a bit of a song, "Summertime
　　　an' the livin' is easy …"

This summer isn't easy but I'm resting in the hammock
　　　of Your care, Lord, living in the reality
　　　of Your presence as I pack and show the house.
To-do lists grow longer by the day.
Time to do them grows shorter.
St. Peter's words rise among my jumbled thoughts,
　　　"Cast your cares on Him for He cares for you."

Yes! Here they are, Lord, my bundle of worries,
　　　inadequacies and problems.
I'm giving them to You with trust as the woman
　　　in the hammock trusts the safety of the ropes.
I don't know how our many "musts" will fit
　　　the time frame but this I know,
Your guidance is like a flashlight illuminating shadows,
　　　showing the right direction.

Father, I have two options, don't I? I can sweat and fret,
　　　or as Your daughter I can exercise my right
　　　to trust You with each day of my future.
I choose the latter. Yes!

115

He's Already There

Deep sloping woods, I shall miss you.
Your moods and seasonal costumes
      speak wonders to my soul.
 Long, leafy tunnels call, "Come, walk my length.
Open all senses to what God has done."

In spring you fling on a lacy mantilla,
      wearing it with graceful charm.
Breeze stirs fragrance of growing things.
Blossoms spring up, splashing brown earth
      with color and new hope.

In summer time your greenness is patterned
      by sunshine and shadow.
Clear birdsong and rustle of furry creatures
      dining on God's provender
      provide background music.

Cool fire of autumn's splendor wraps
      about me, leaving me breathless.
Seasonal changes, year after year, are similar
      yet each is unique.
The joy of Creation pumps through me like adrenalin.

Winter's muffling snows tune unsuspecting ears
      to listen to the silence.
Skeleton trees, black by contrast, dance wildly
      as wind takes up her refrain, keening,
      whistling, howling, sobbing.

I shall miss the blazing hearth on fog thick nights
        as flames leap against darkened stone.
Smoke, like transparent velvet, carries an occasional
        living spark up the chimney.

It's time to say another goodbye before we move
        to a place where river and sea lie side by side.
But this is my Father's world,
        I'm not saying goodbye to Him.
I'm only saying hello to Florida
        for He is already there.

Skipping Years

Today I'm skipping years, which we may do
    only after they have passed.
We may bring to mind whatever we wish
    or delete the unwanted.
Neither present nor future grant this privilege.
Today I choose to skip five decades.

Christmas Eve brings a jolly daddy dressed
    in white whiskers and rented red suit
    to the hearth at Springdale.
He ho-ho-hos and pats small heads
    while drawing wee gifts from a big black bag.
Our tiny Kakie, nephew Mark and son Bill,
    keep eyes riveted on the season's elf,
    absorbing each detail of the show.

Later while Bill sleeps under his covers
    and sugar plums dance in his dreams,
    a seed sprouts quietly ...
Aha! That big elf is none other our Dad!
The real Santa could wear a ring
    embossed with North Pole College
but ...there's no possibility he would be wearing
    a ring from Emory University!

It Ends With a Beginning

Wake up! Wake up! An old year's passing
    on tired feet, with cares untold.
So much occurred which can't be righted,
    people neglected, unfinished projects …
    learn from them.

Look up, be quick! A new year's speeding
    on shining wheels, transporting hope.
Brand new beginnings, so fresh,
    unencumbered by worries,
    unspoiled by deeds. May it come!

We enter this swift vehicle of necessity
    and speed on.
Regardless of turbulence, One stands beside me.
He is no stranger. We've walked and talked,
    I've fought and run! We've laughed before.
    Let's move on!

My trust is this: He is my Light.
Darkness can't quench Him. He is beside me.
    Why should I fear?
Through all years He has been my Helper.
 His help is never early, never too late.
    May I keep my trust!
                       Amen